The Frog Princess

Coloring book

AUTHOR AND ILLUSTRATOR
OLGA GOLOVESHKINA

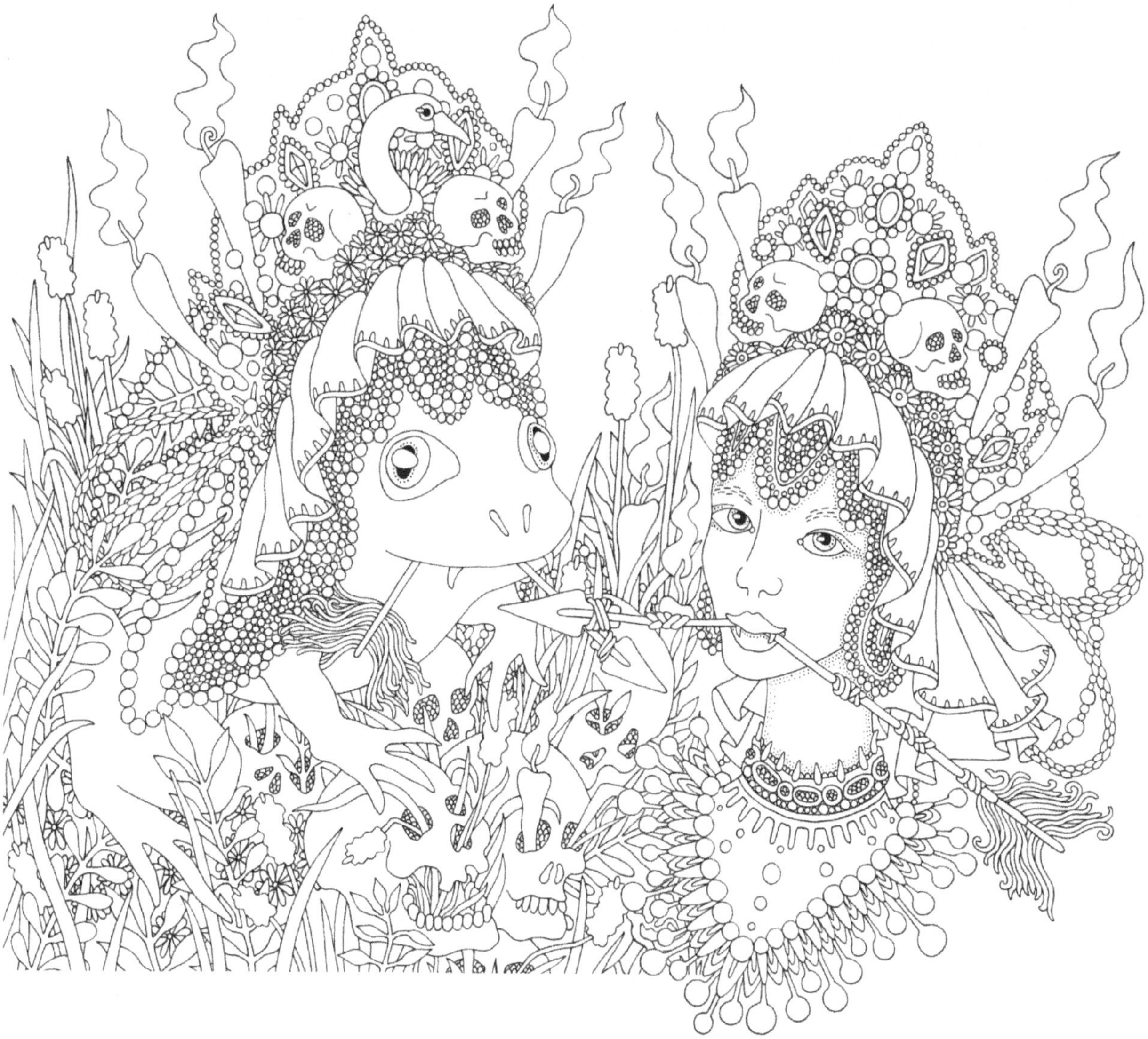

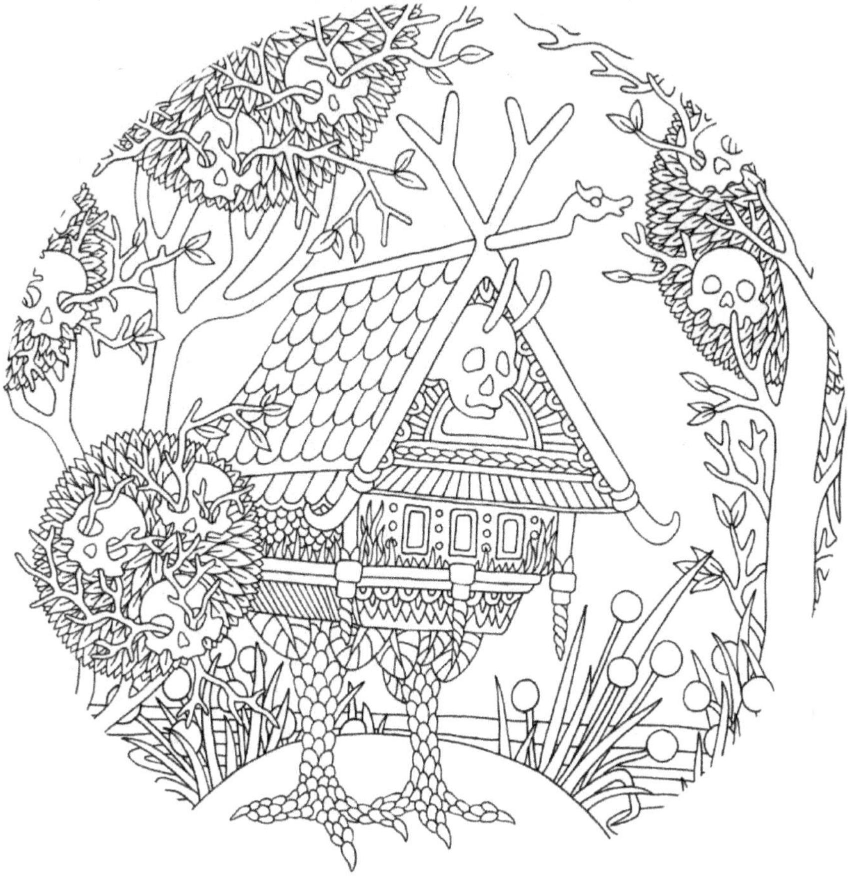

This book belongs to

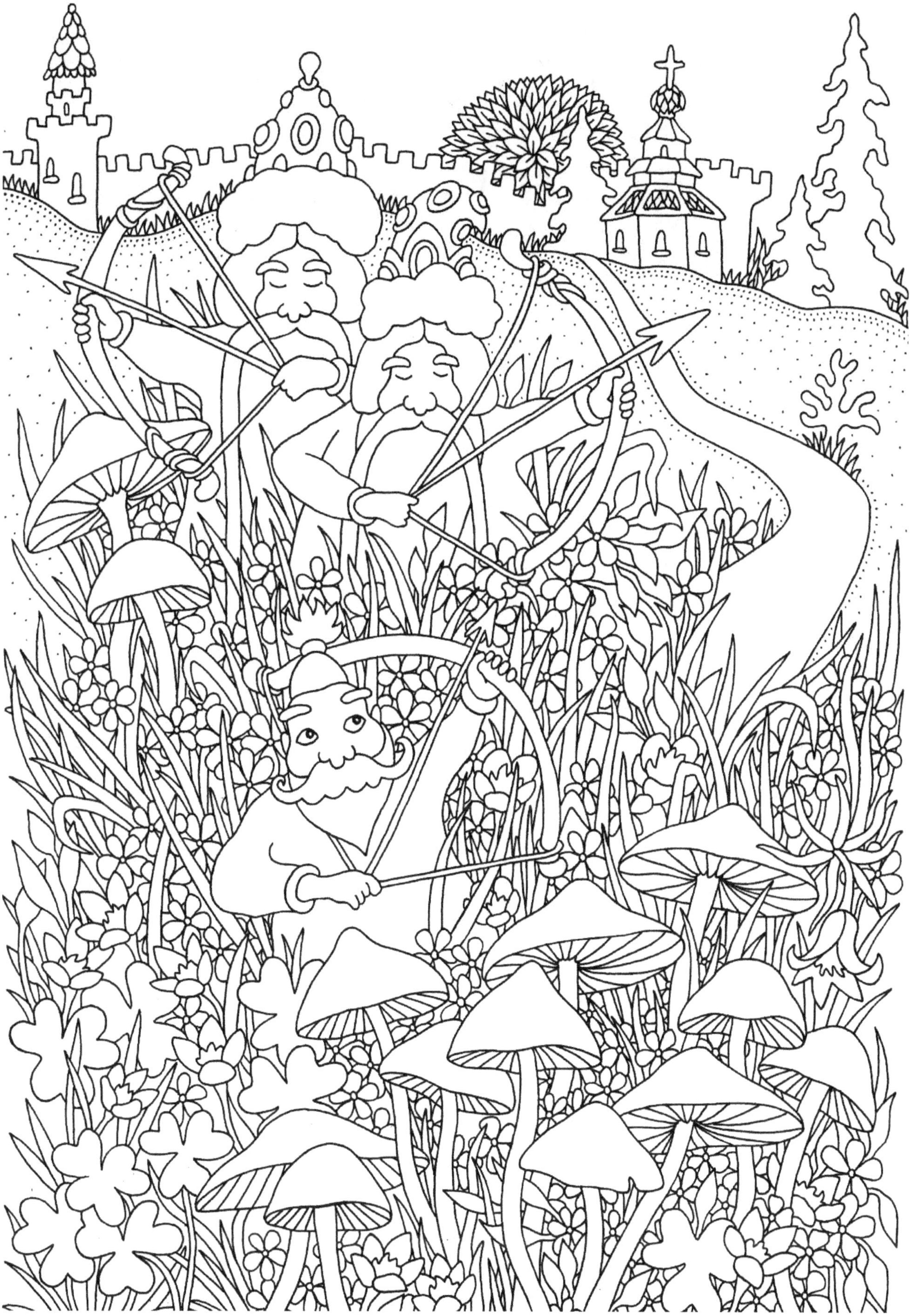

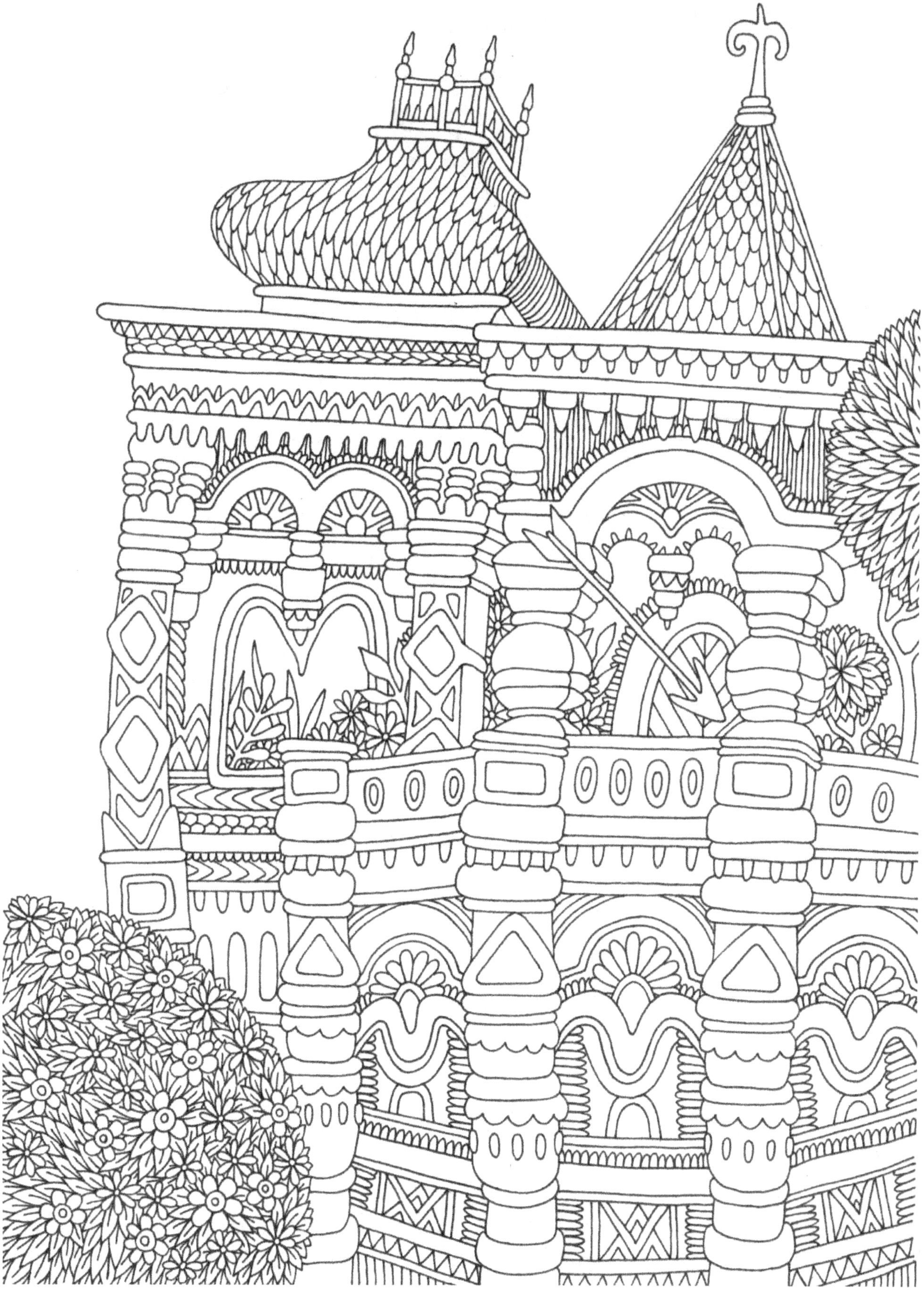

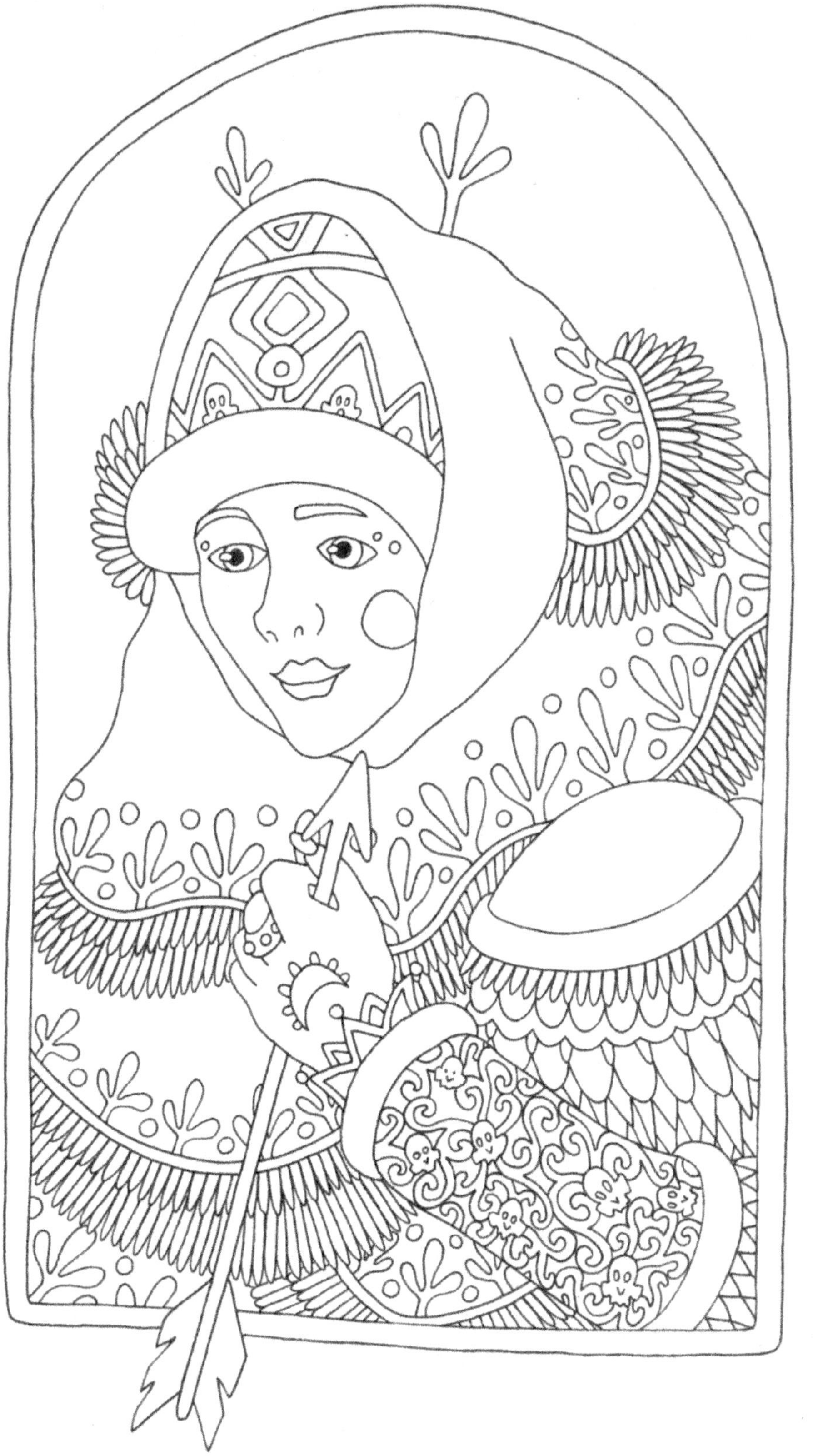

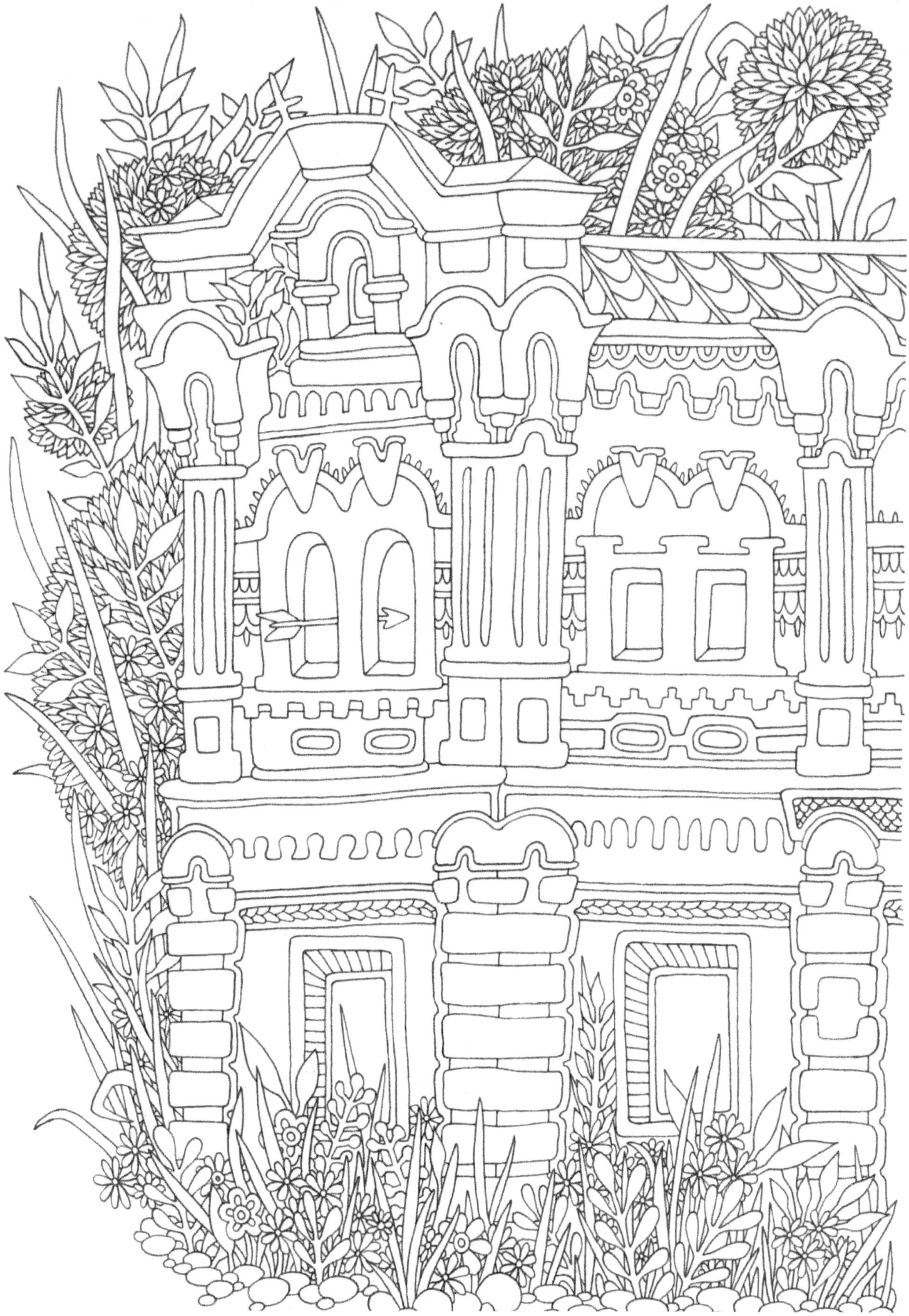

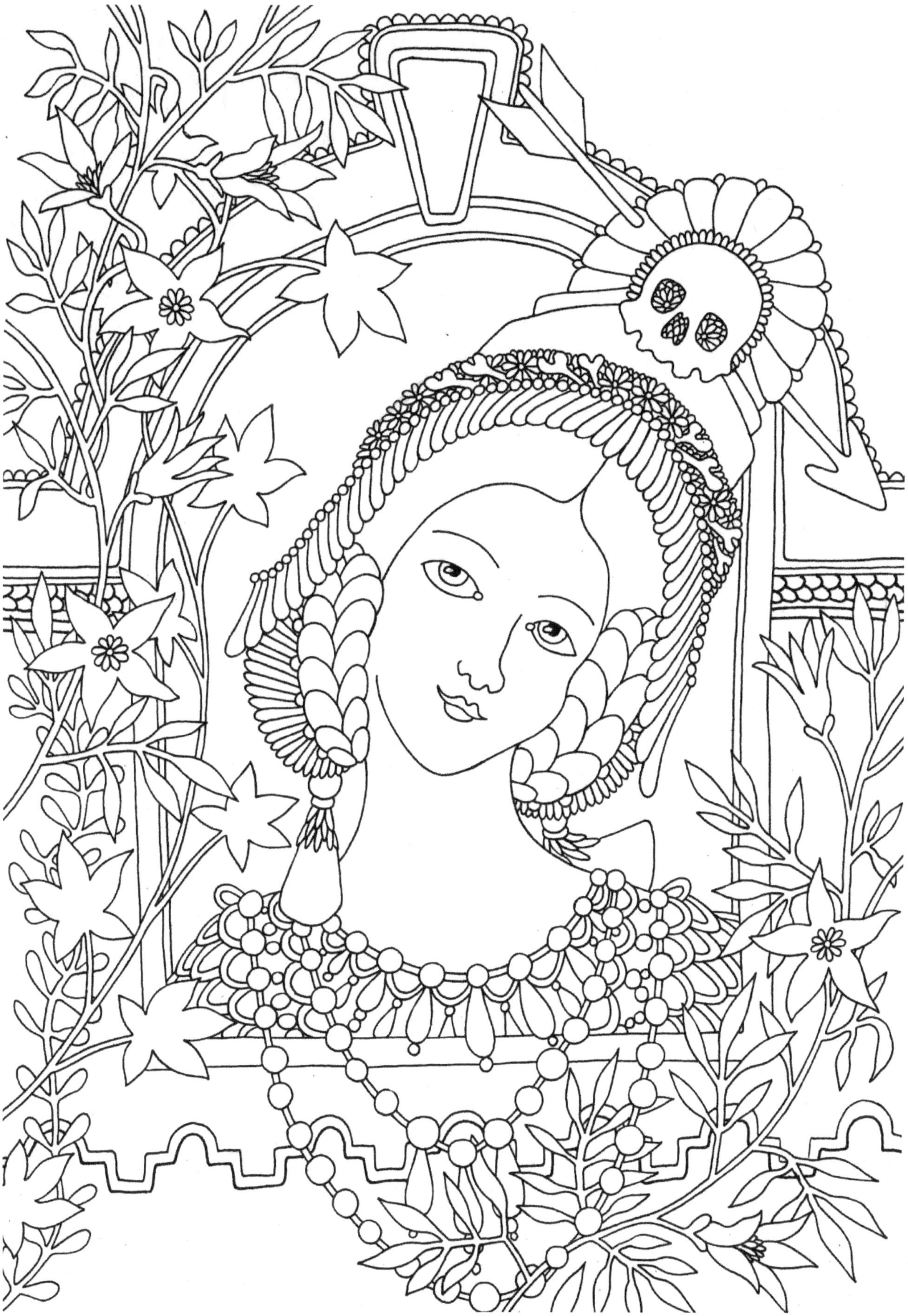

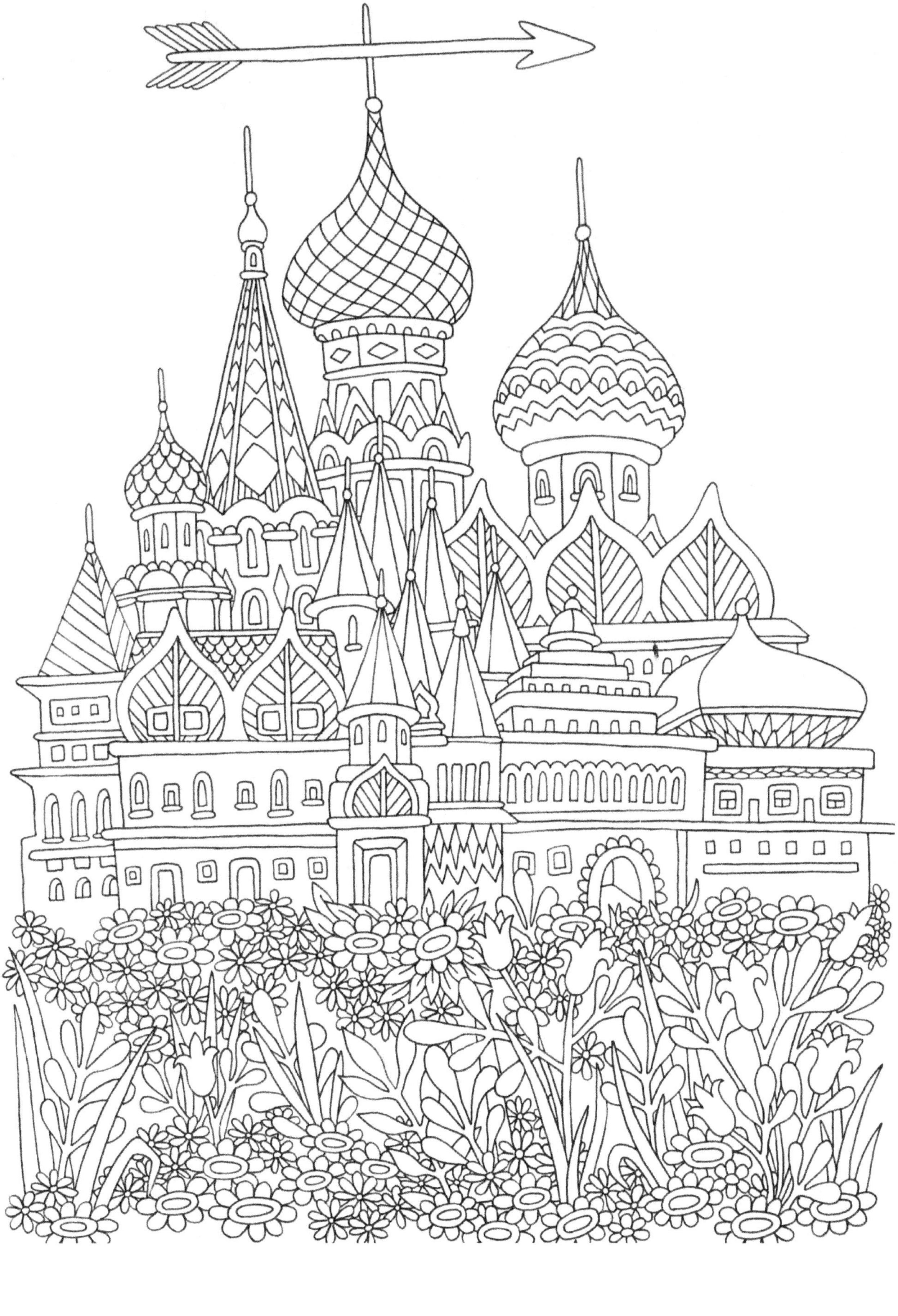

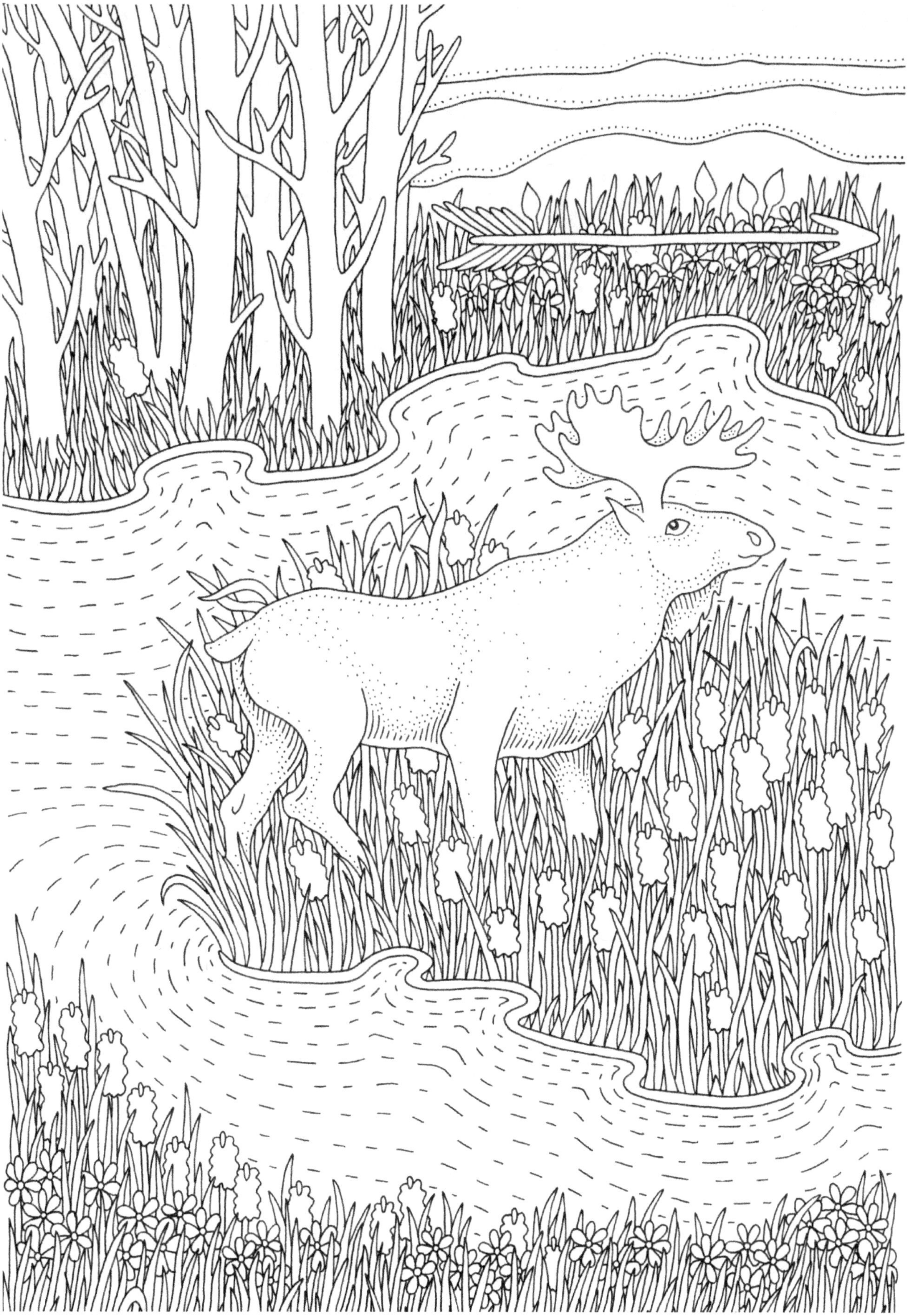

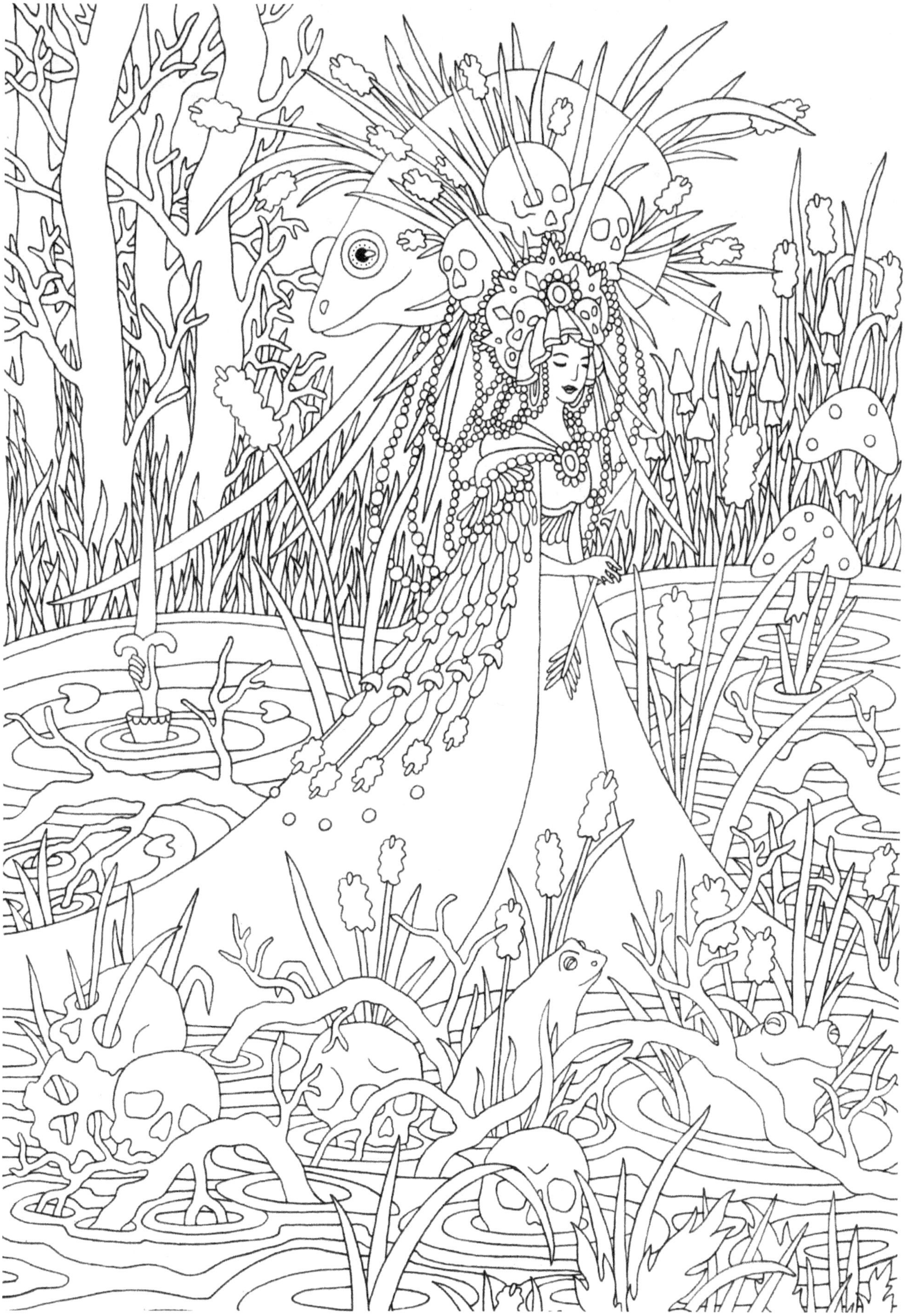

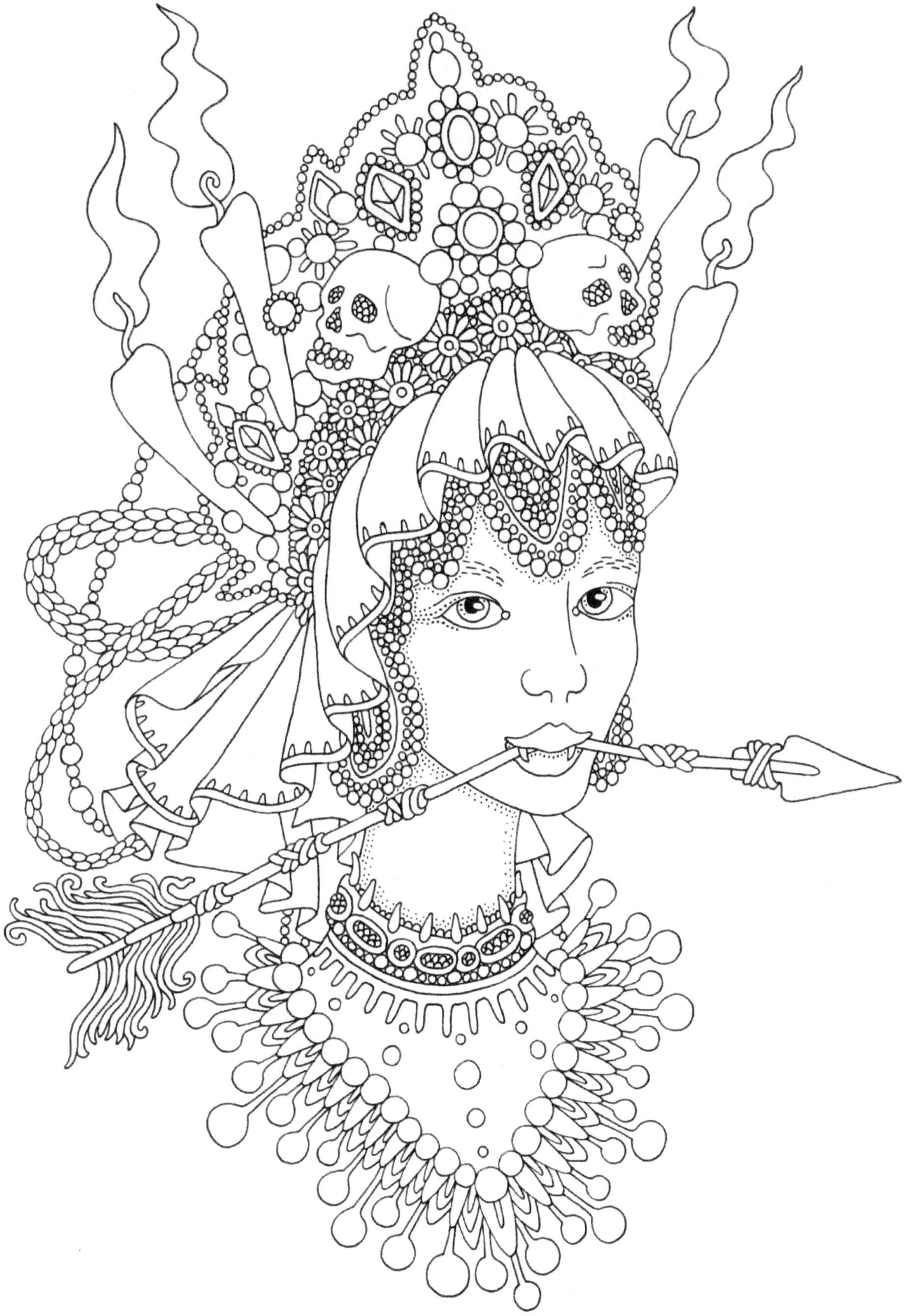

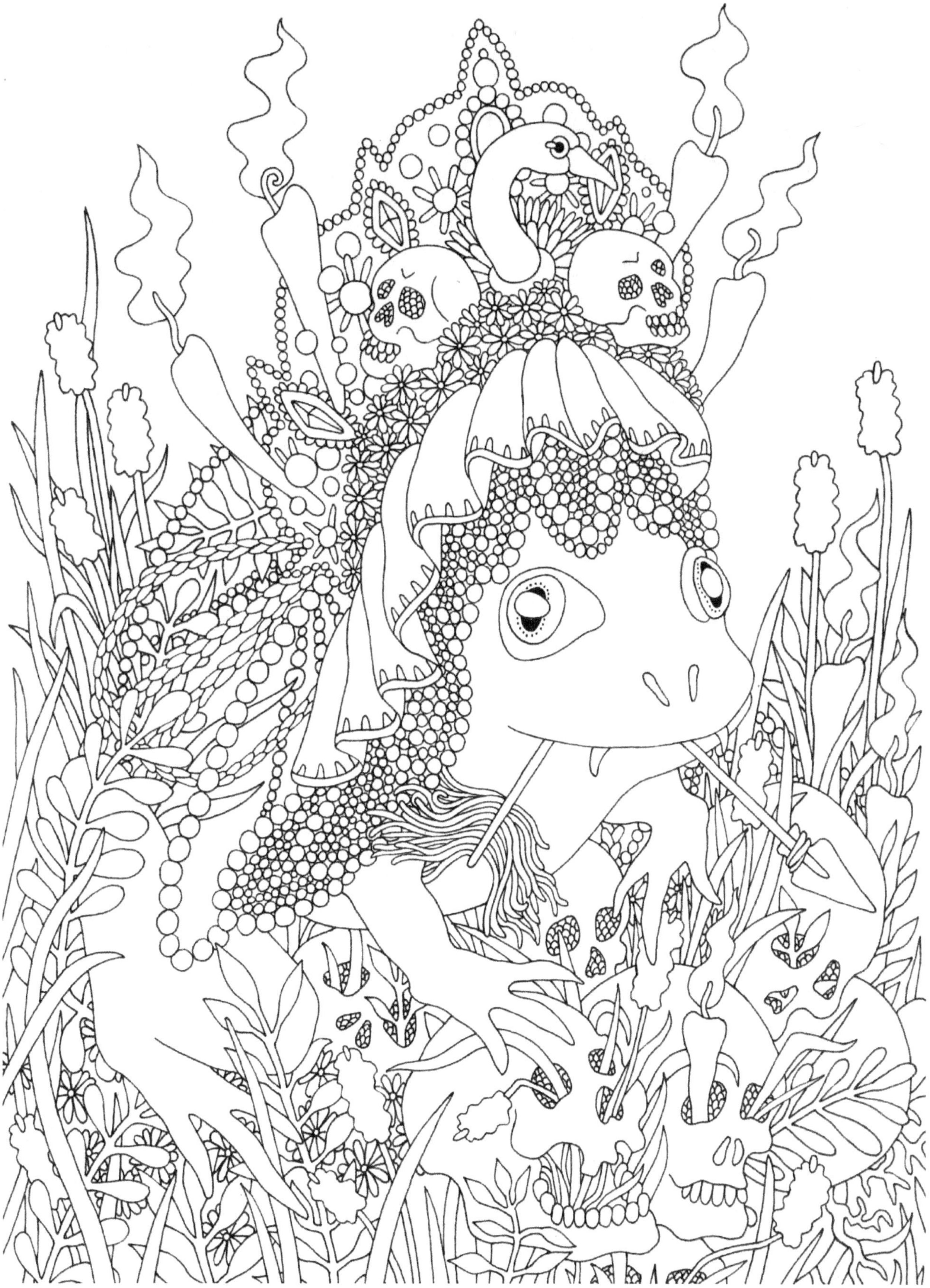

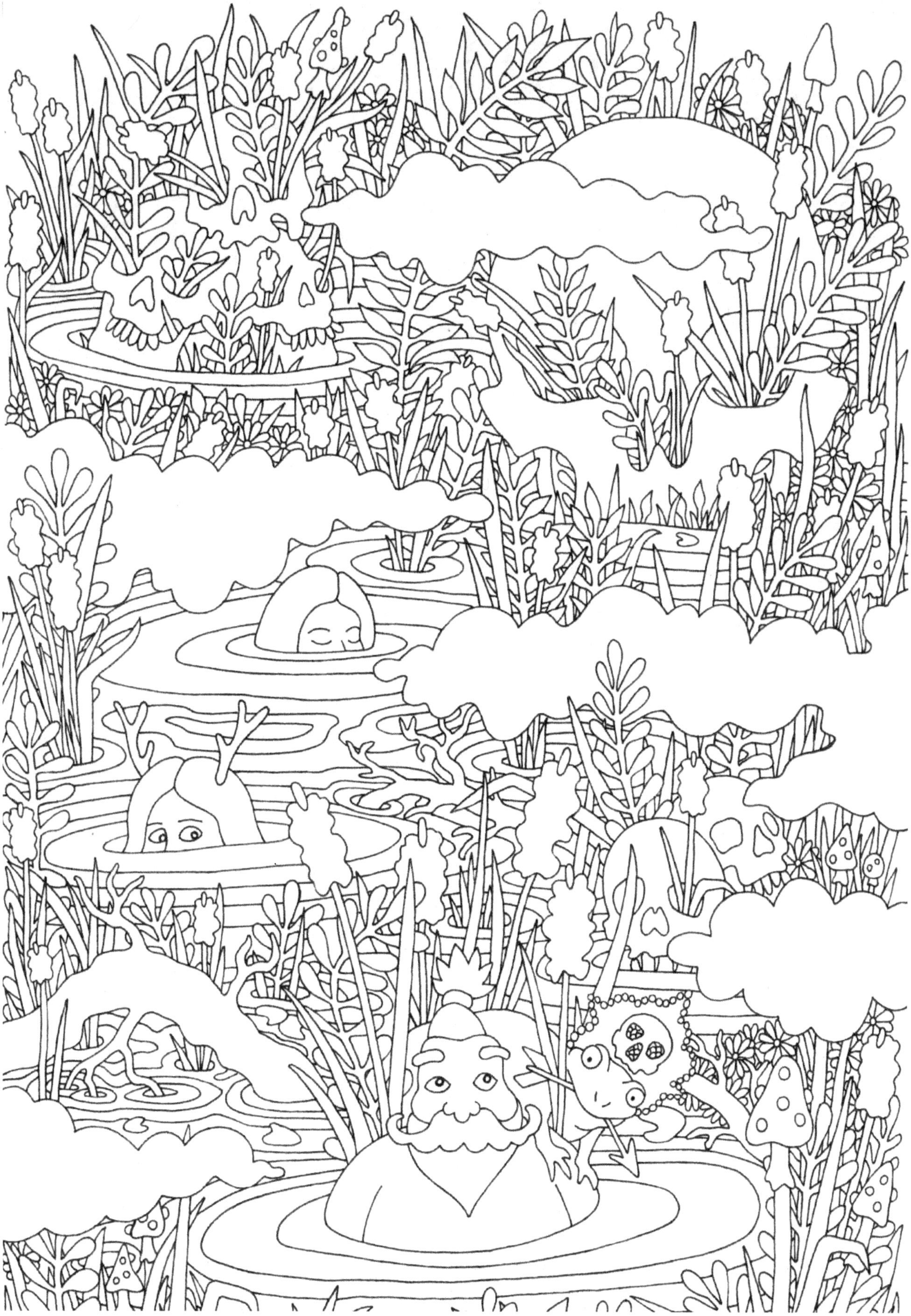

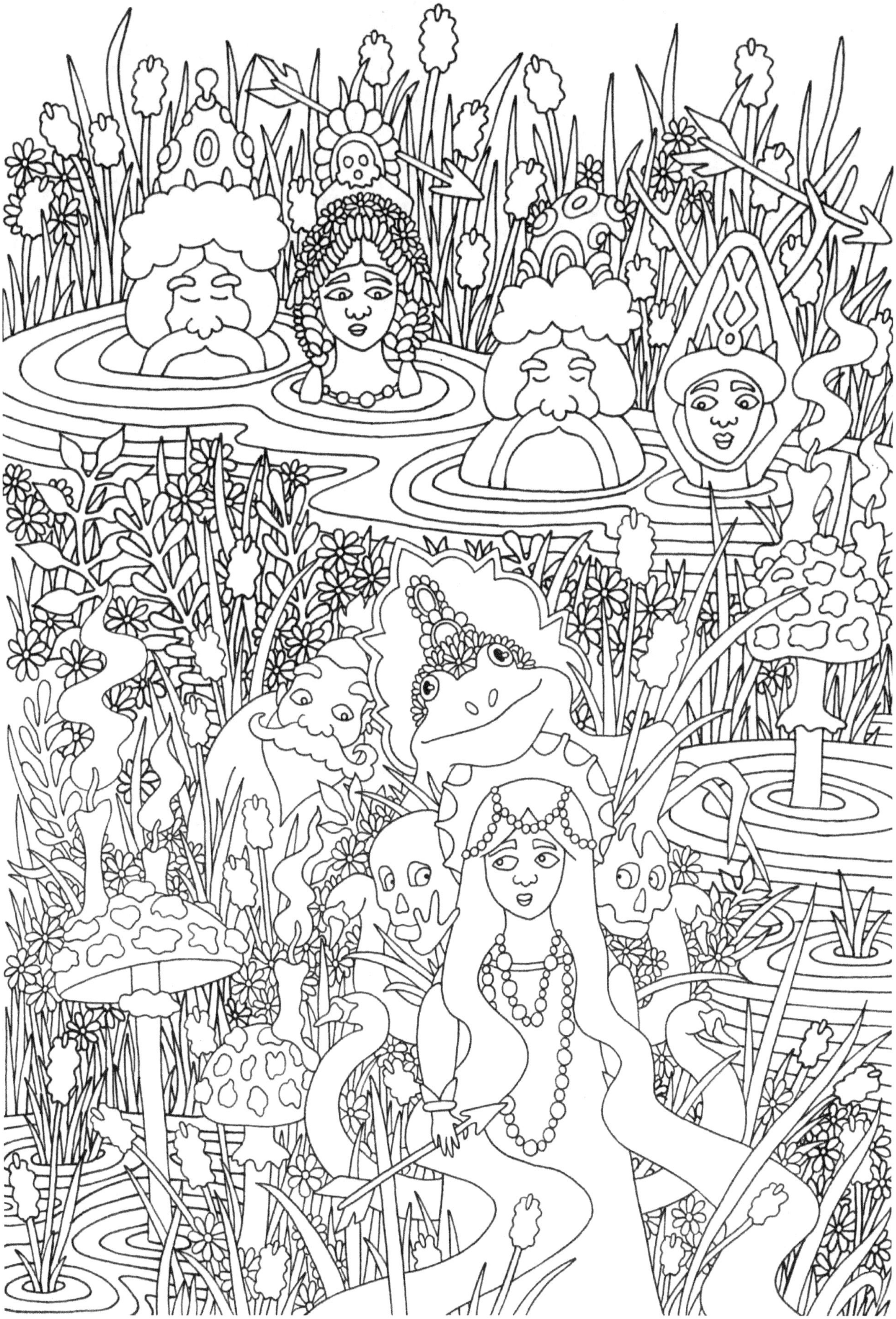

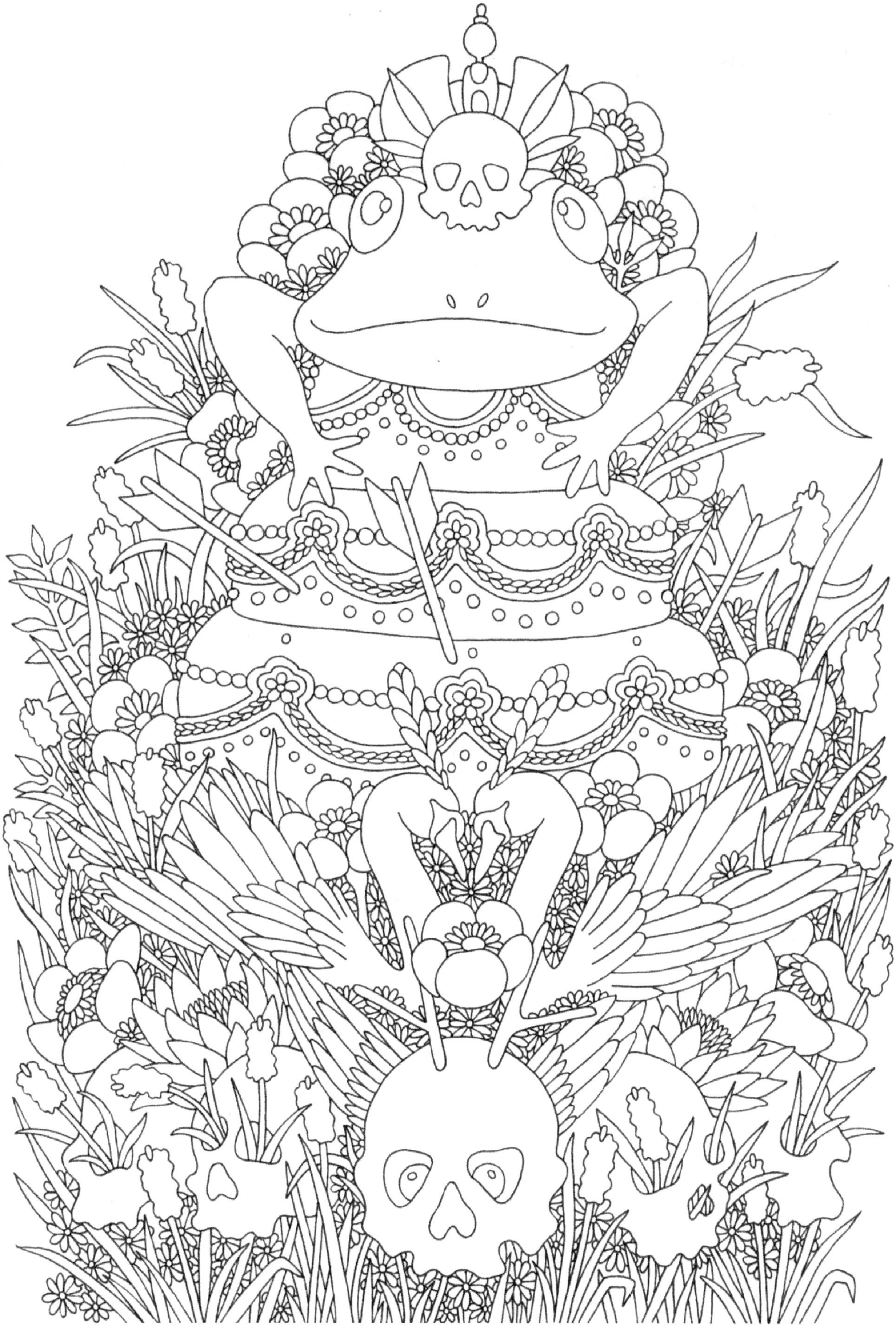

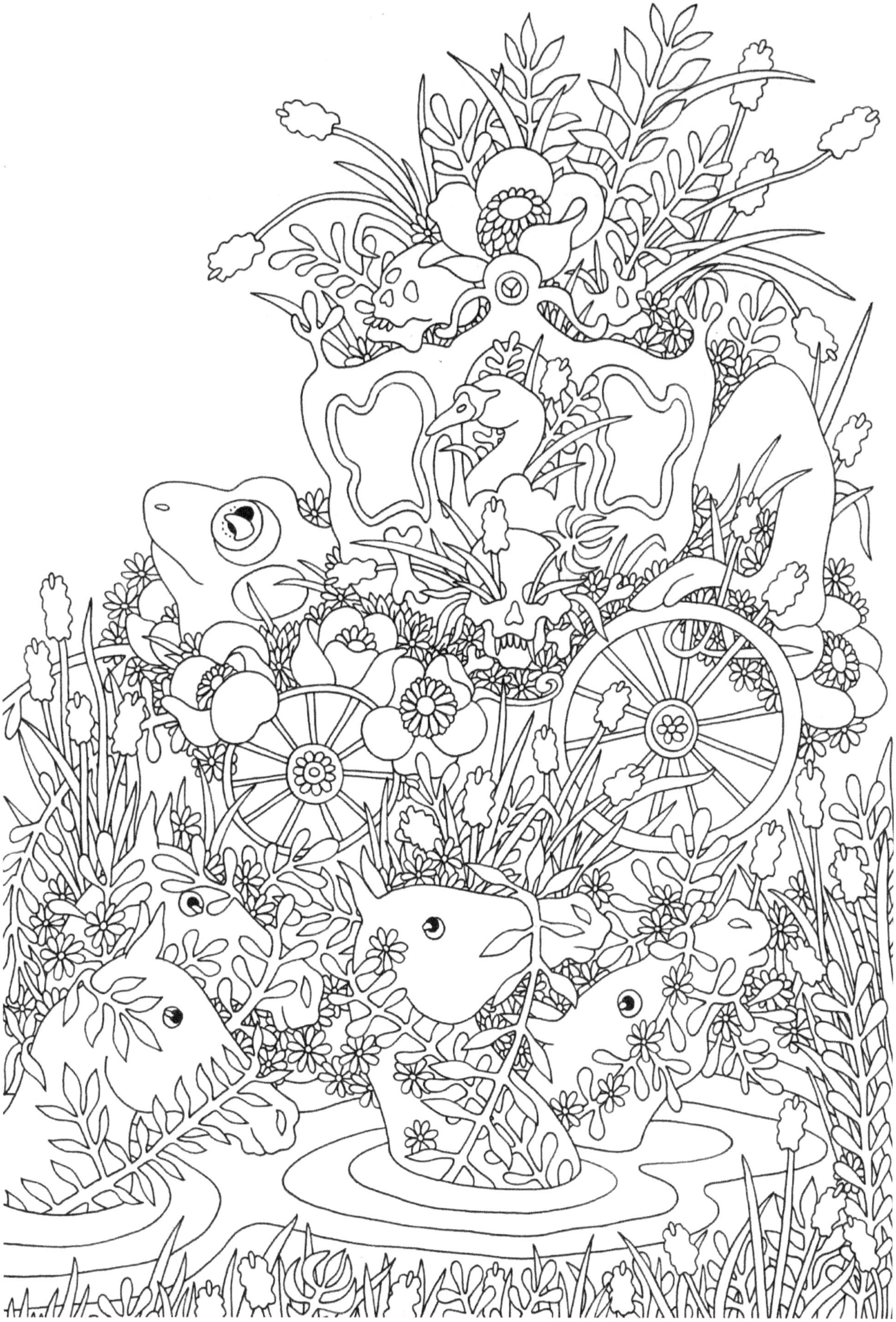

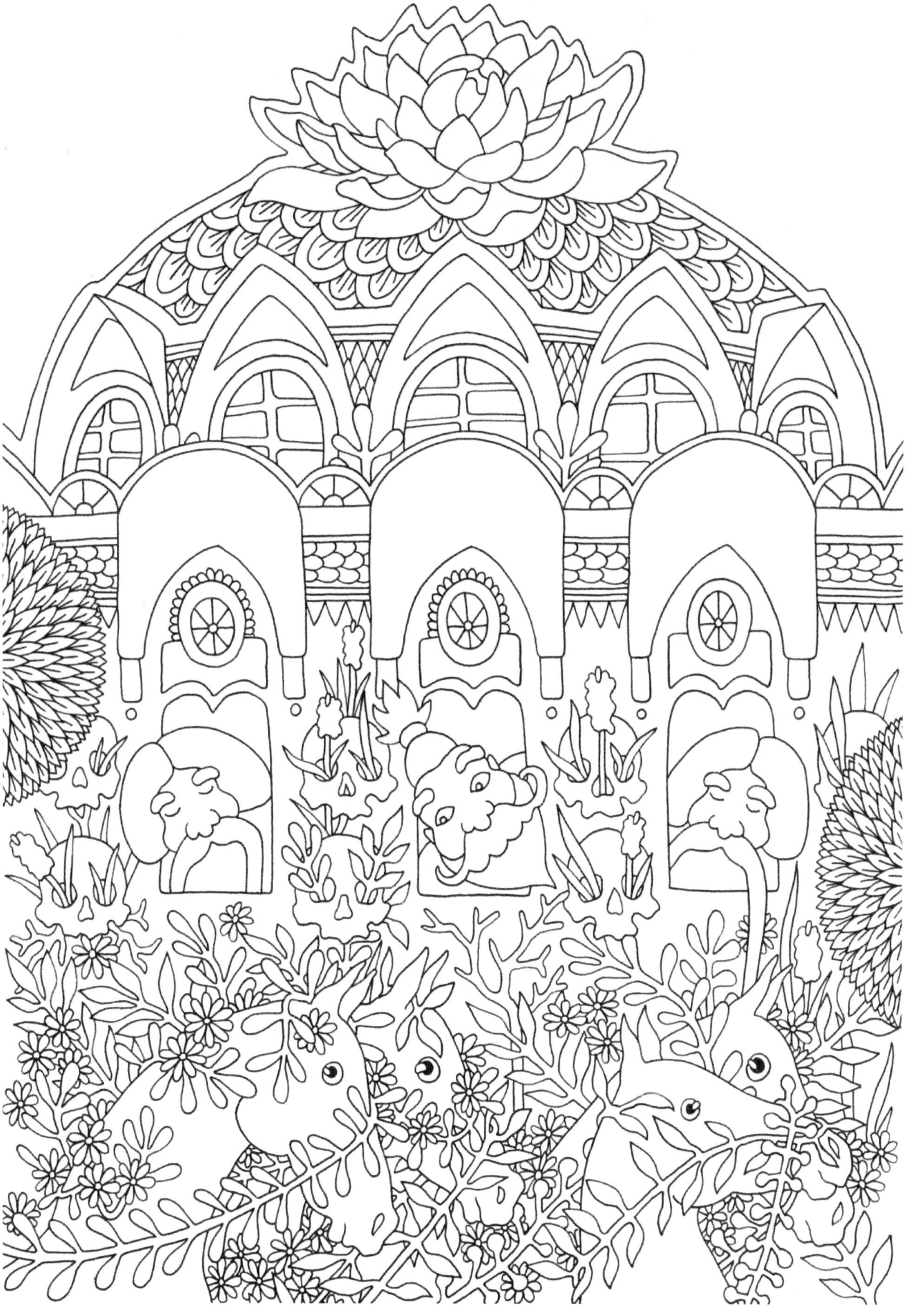

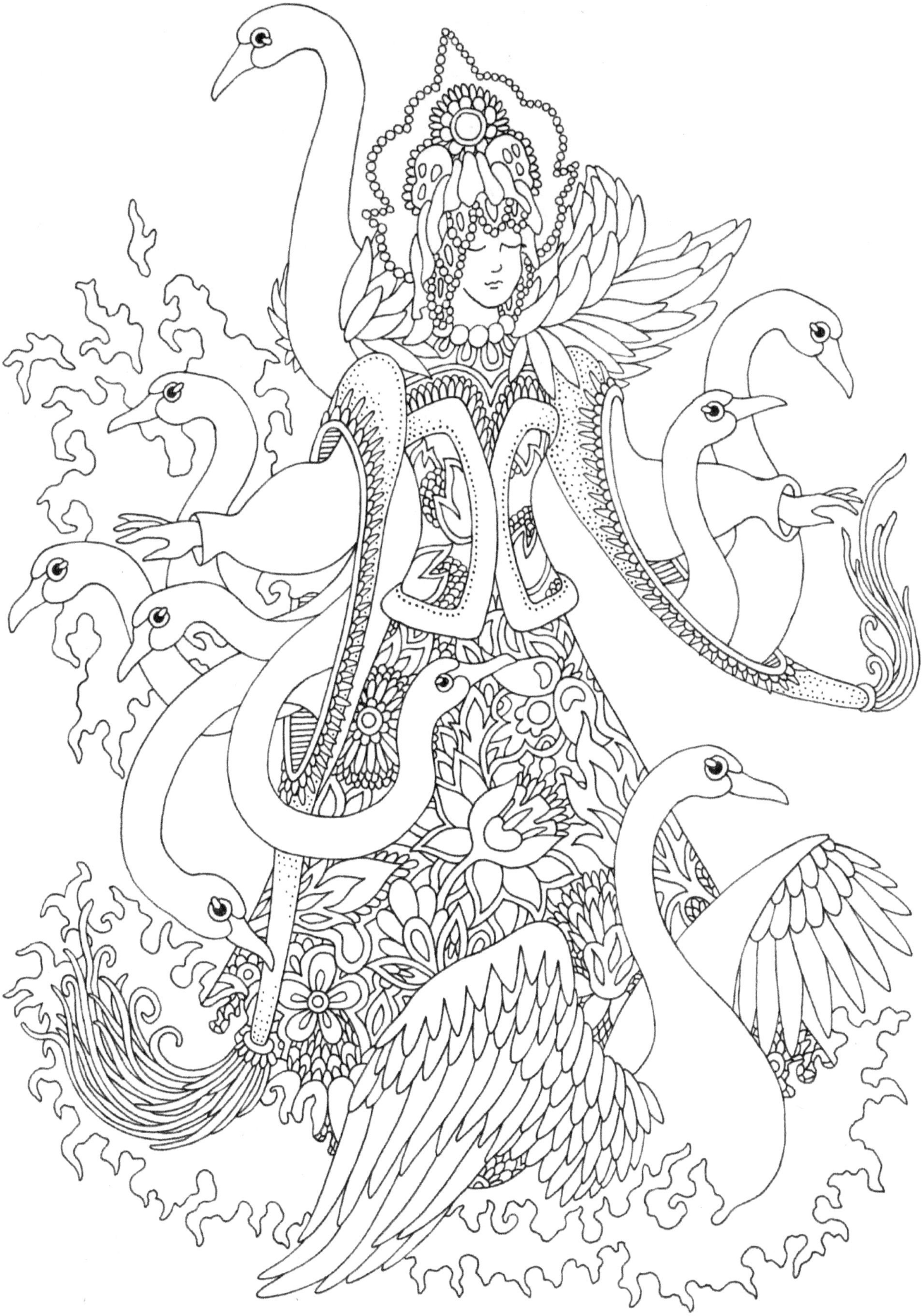

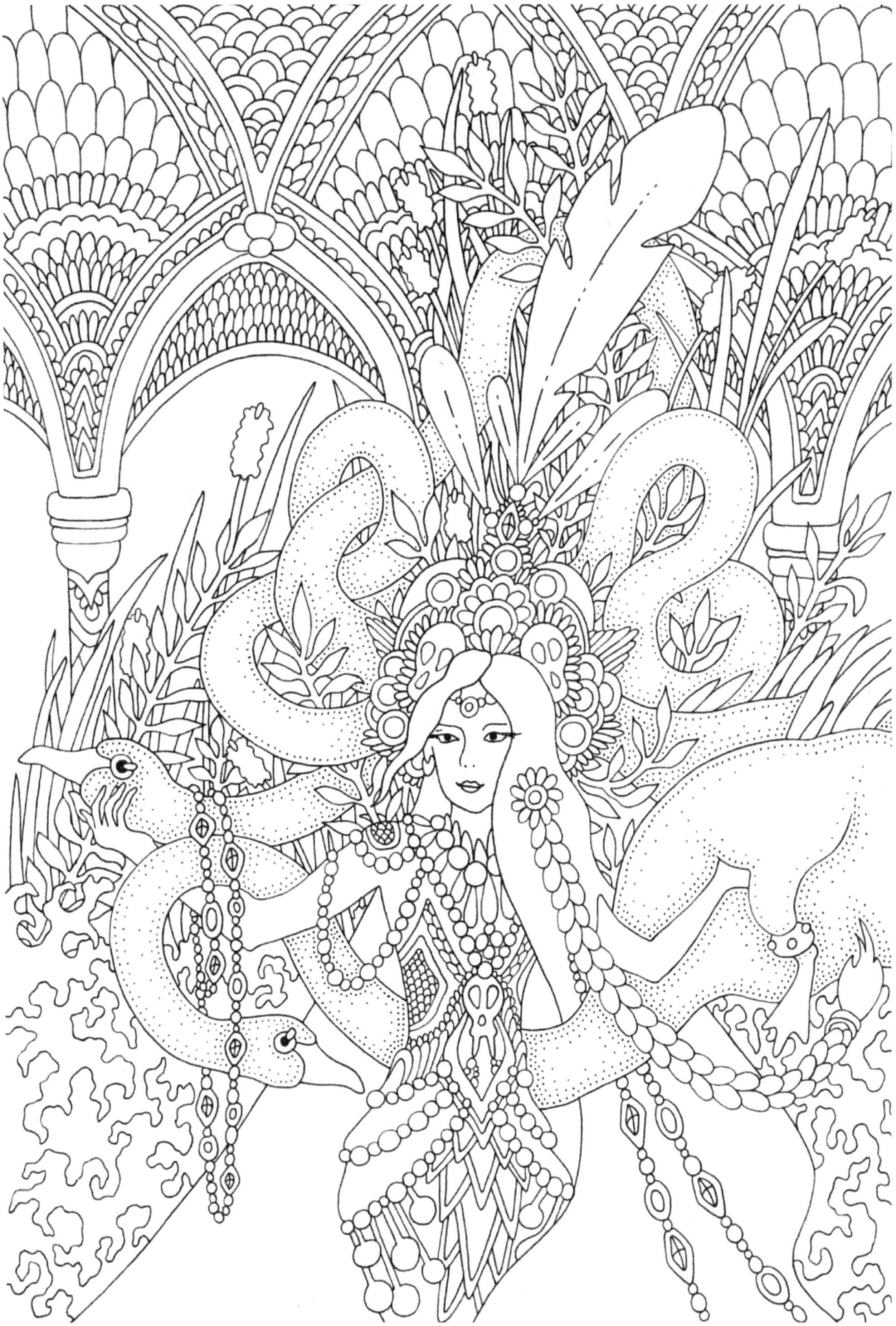

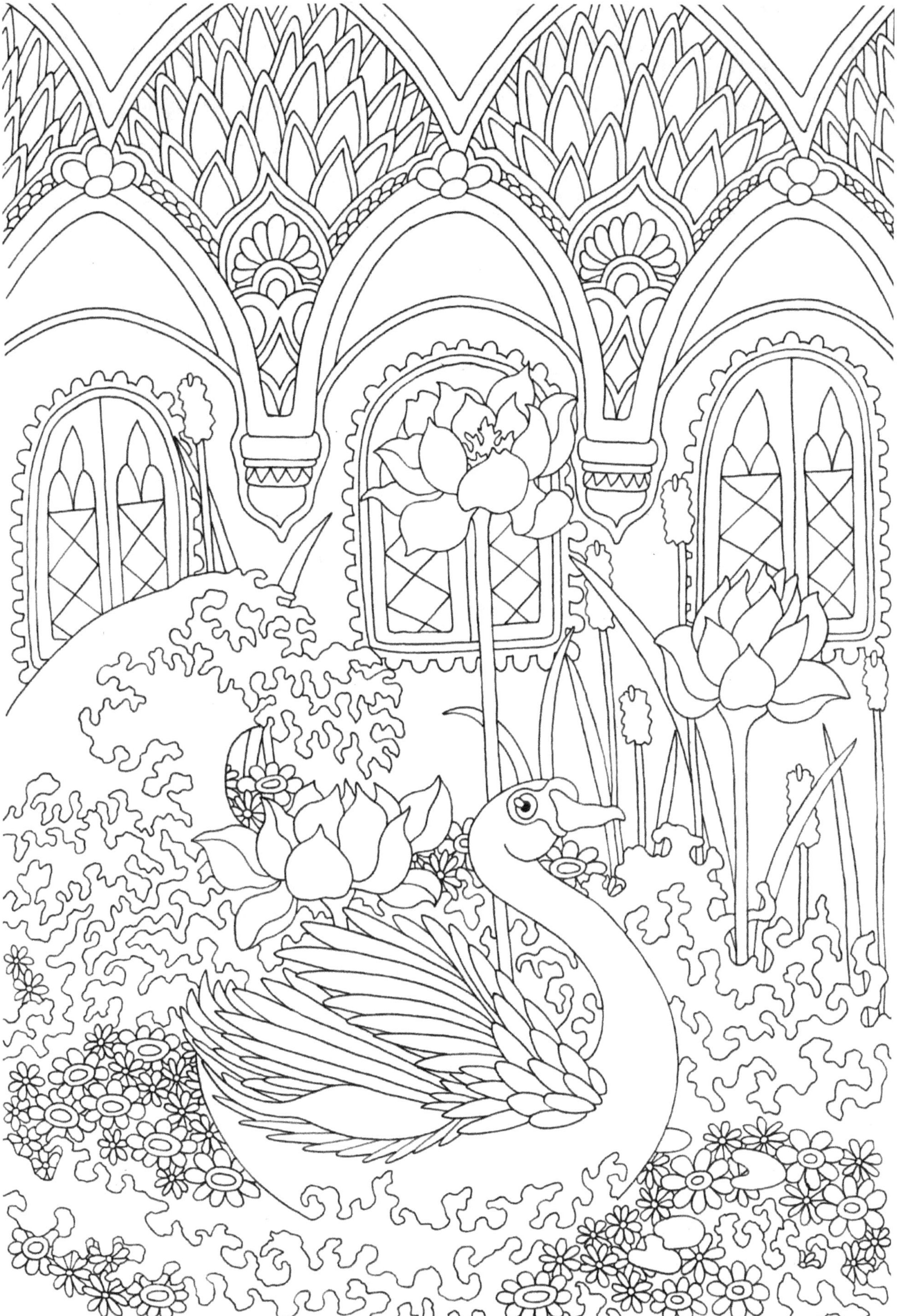

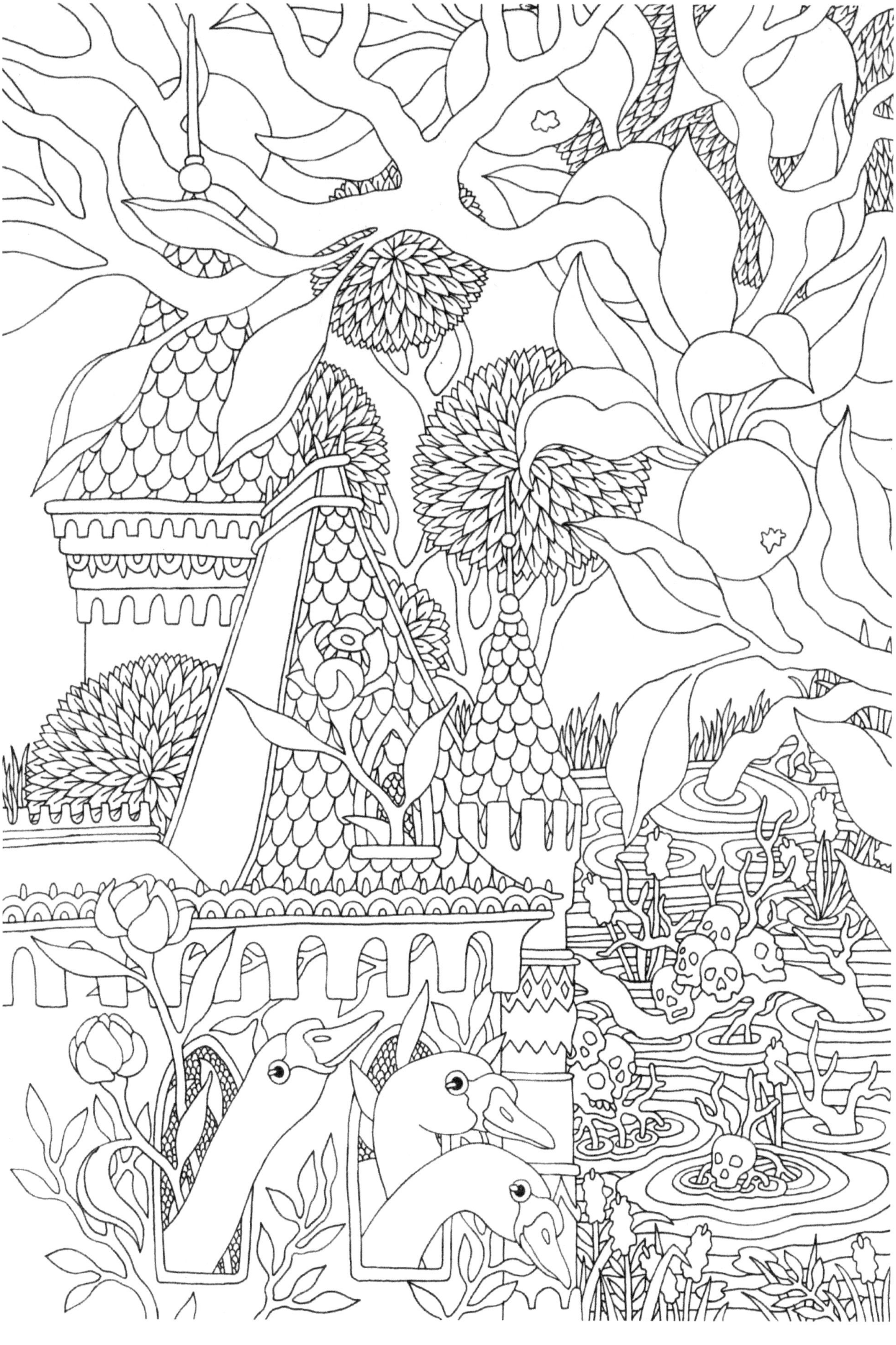

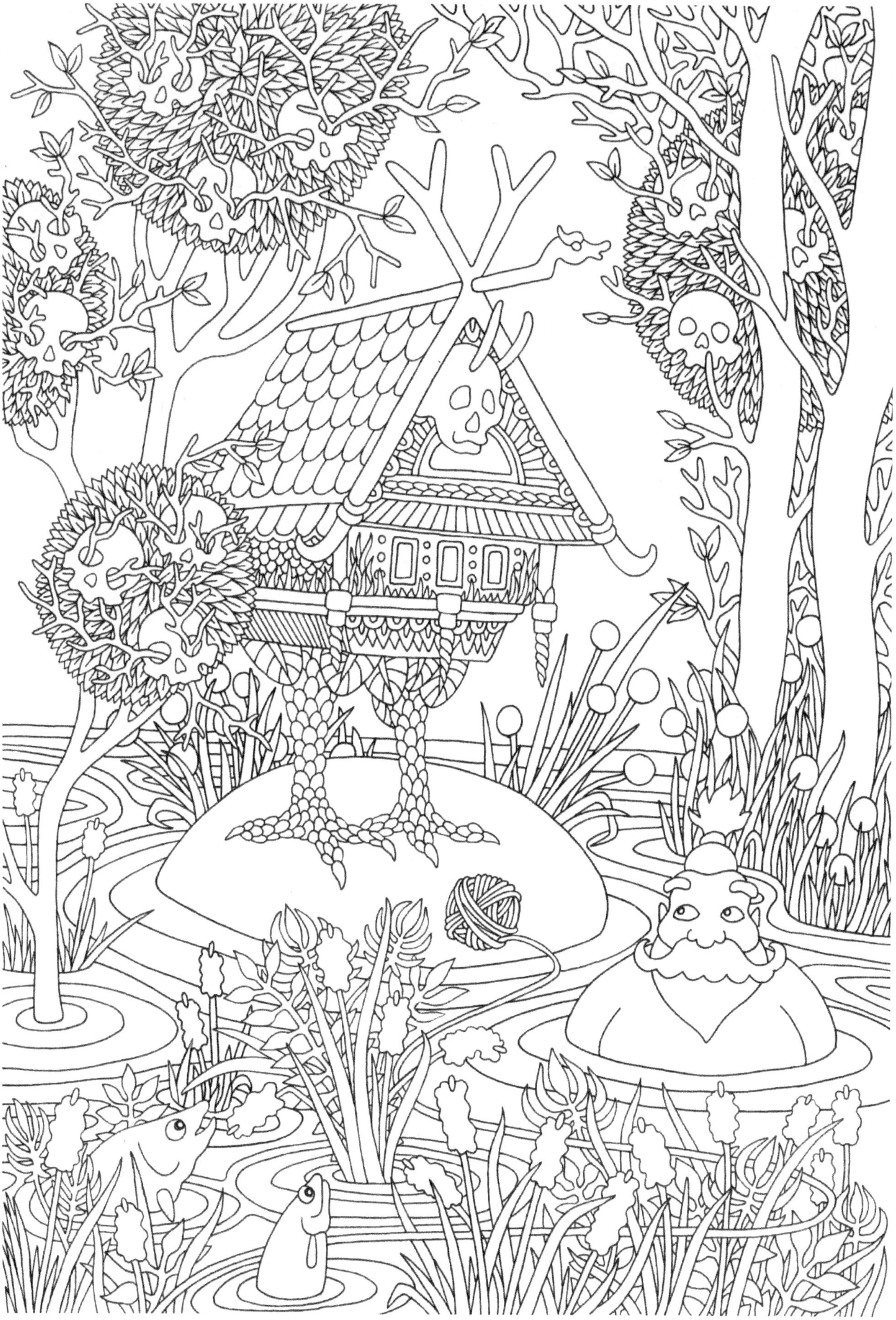

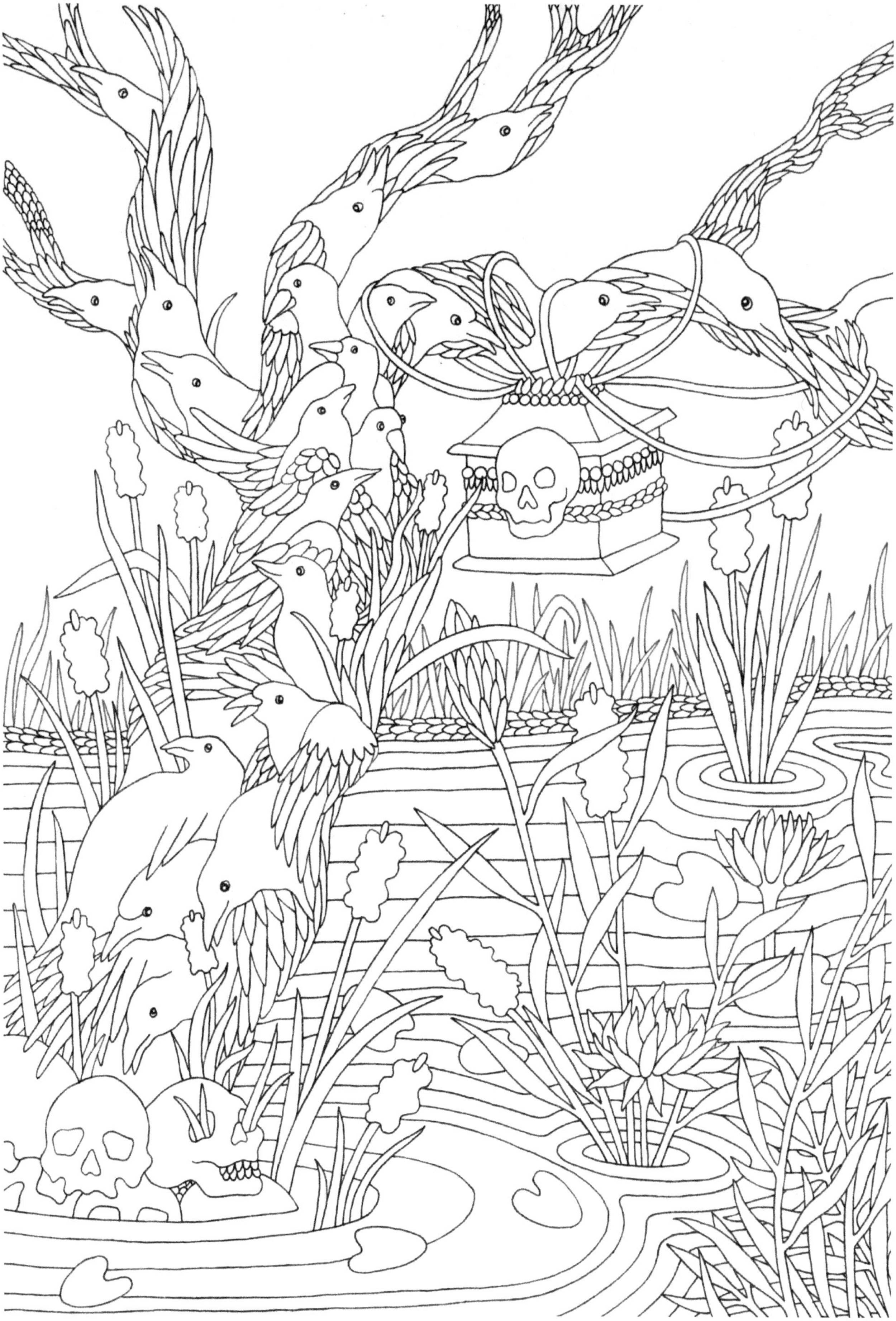

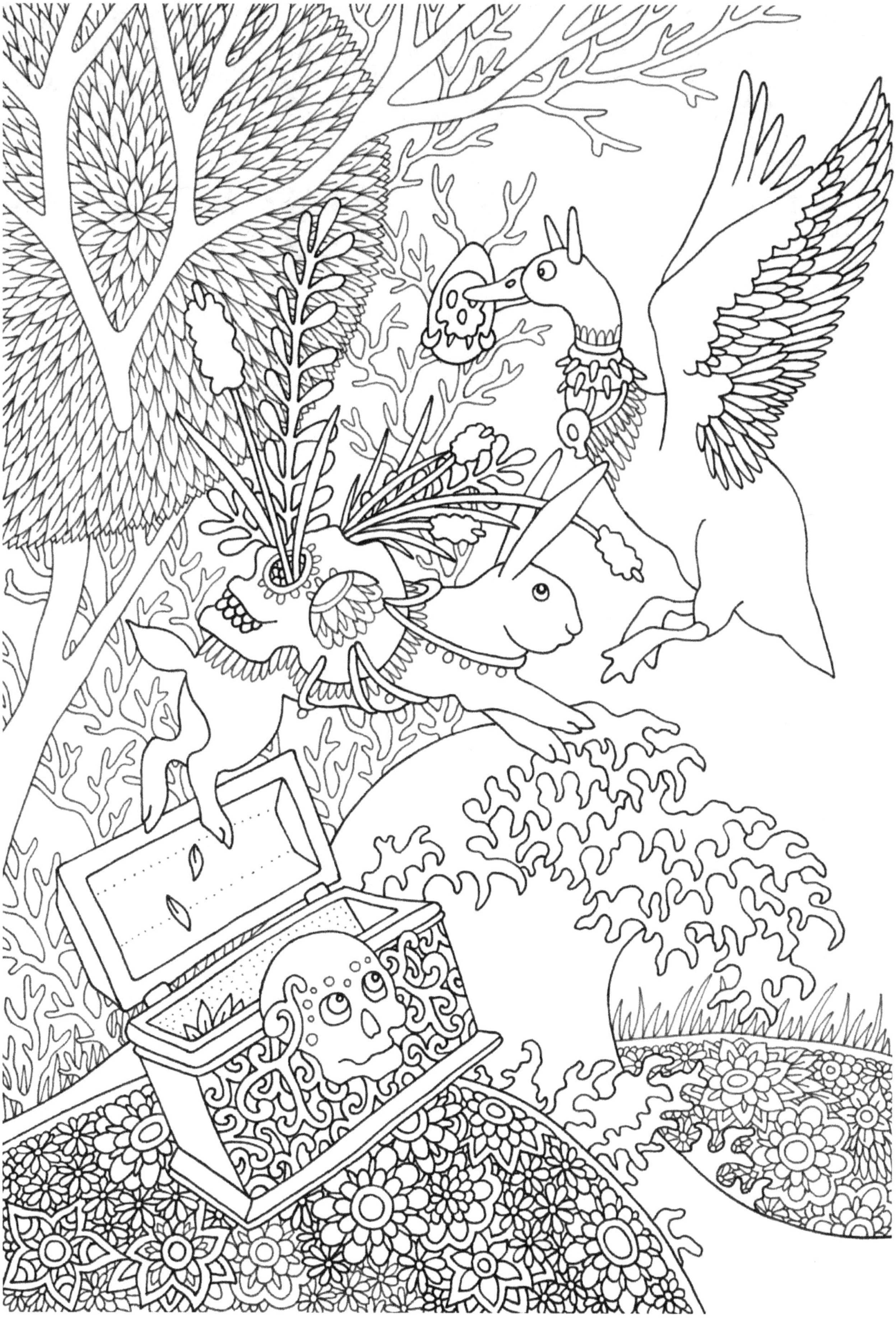

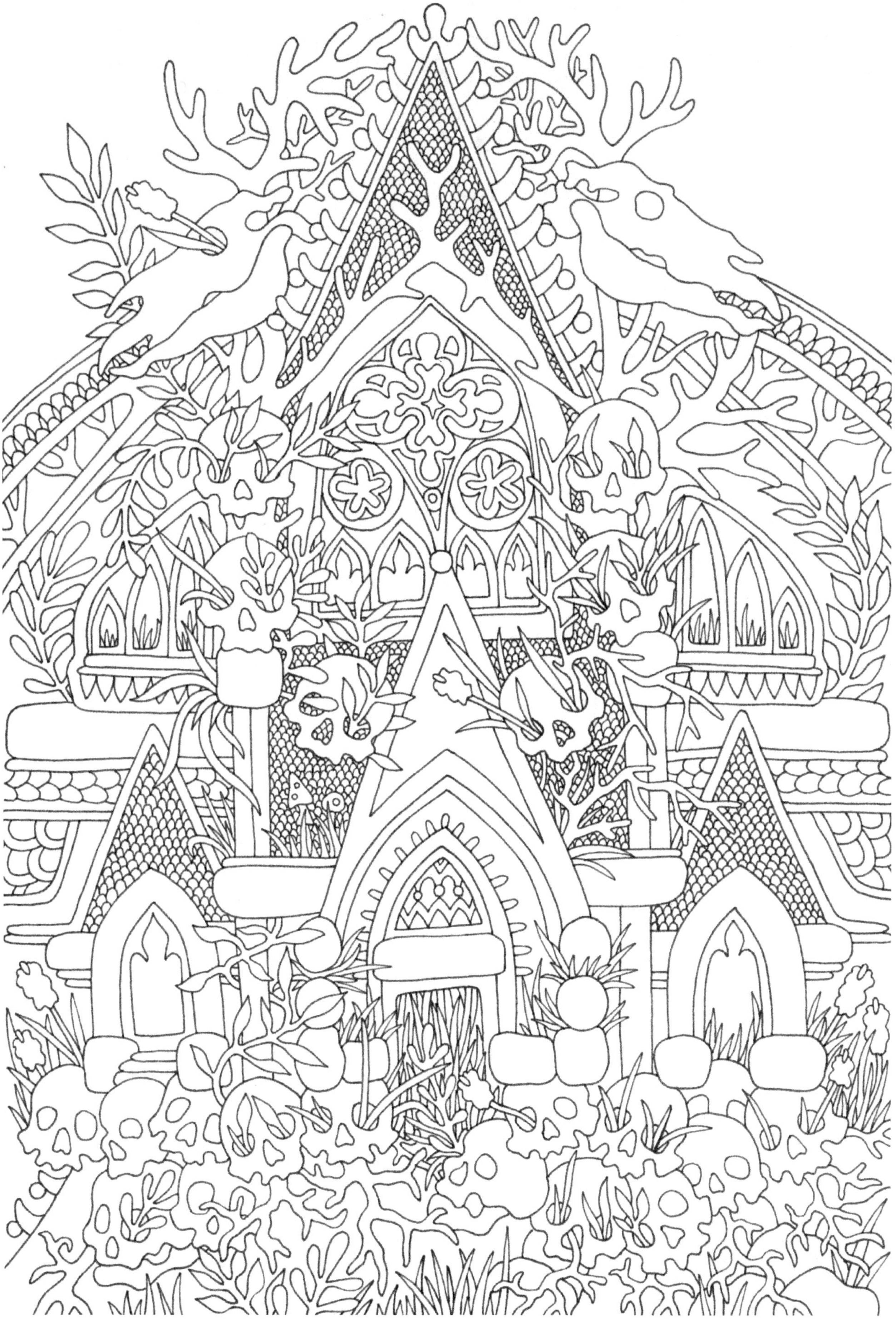

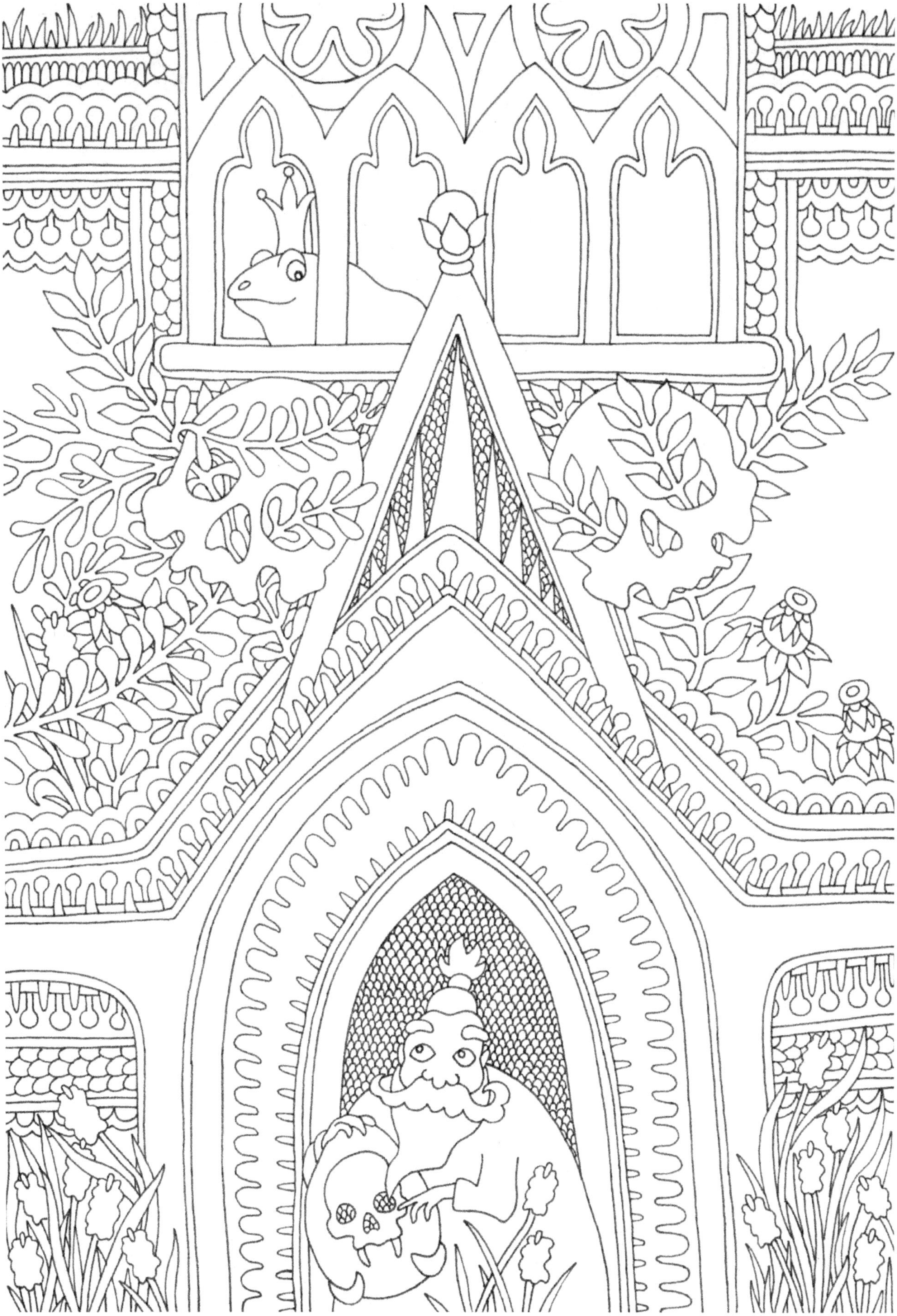

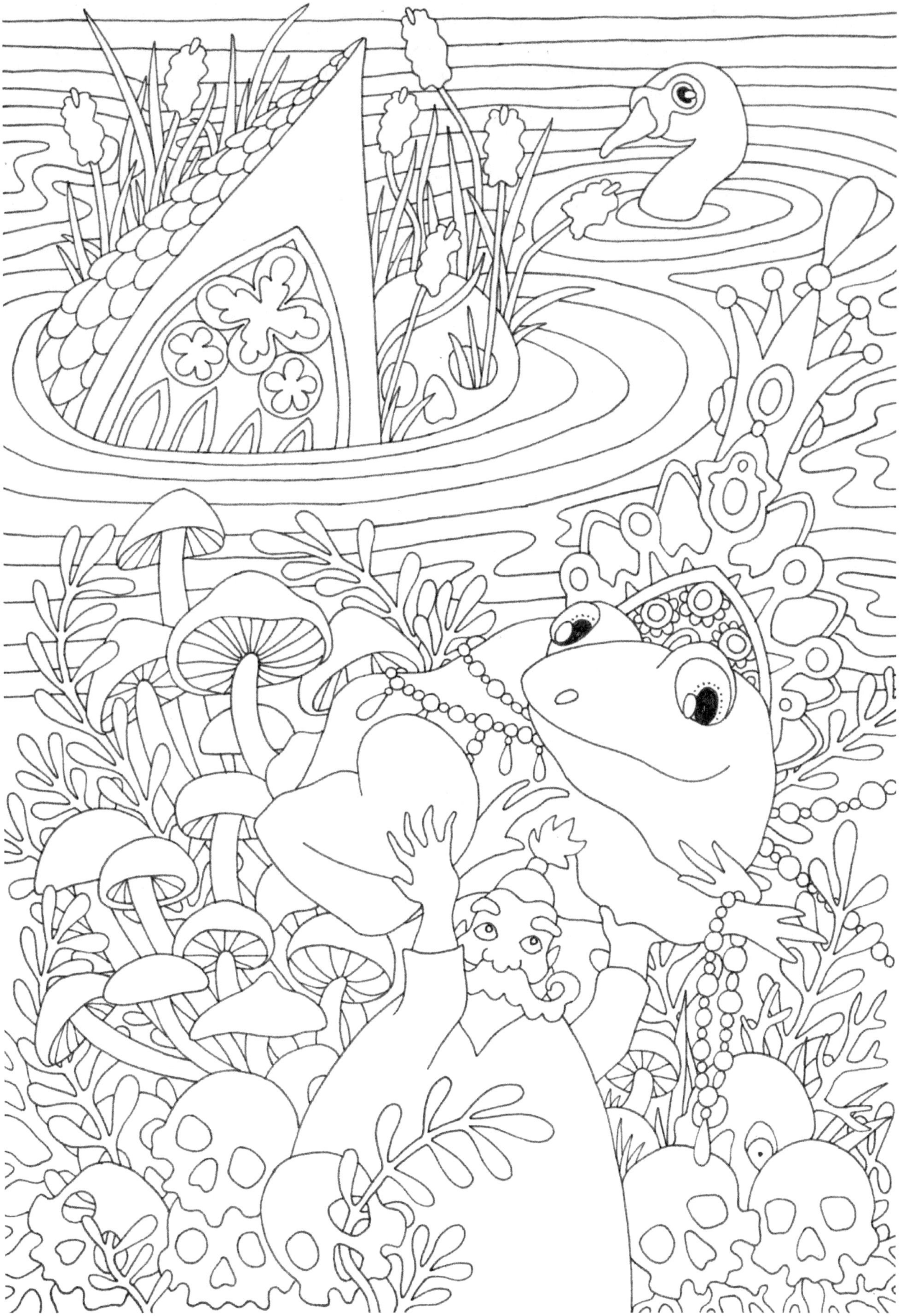